For Tylan Marie, as cute as can be...

Intro to Chakras

Do you know that you are full of stars?

Do you know that you are full of stars? A funny thought, I know, but it happens to be true. You see, the same ingredients God used to create the stars is also shining brightly inside of you.

Wheels of light called Chakras spin and dance all through your beautiful body. Eight energy center beginning just below your feet, moving upward through your body, and ending with the last Chakra at the top of your head.

Have you ever heard the expression "You're a great big bundle of energy?" Has anyone ever said that about you? Well, that is what you are. Each Chakra has a brilliant color that vibrates to spin and spread energy. Each Chakra has a special purpose that transmits kind of like electricity, sending out and receiving information. It is this energy that makes you feel alive. Understanding the uniqueness of each Chakra and learning to be "in communica- tion" with the messages your body is sending out can give you a sense of personal power. Thinking of your self as an energy being can allow you to con- sciously manage your personal power and provide you with a greater sense of health and well being.

As you learn to listen to the subtle messages of your body, you will begin to build confidence in your own natural ability to know what your Spirit needs. Chakras are wonderful gifts, and awareness of your bodies energy systems can enable you to trust in your own inner wisdom an know that true guidance is found within.

The Earth Star Chakra

We all have the same support system, the same Mother... EARTH!

The first Chakra in your energy field rests just below your feet, and is called the Earth Star, the color is usually a shade of brown or black. The Earth Star Chakra allows us to feel connected to the plants, animals, faeries, and of course, to Mother Earth. You might envision it as a warm shimmering ball of light. The Earth Star spins gently beneath your feet and brings you a feeling of being "grounded" and connected to nature. What does being grounded feel like? It feels like calm, peaceful, and at ease in your body.

Standing barefoot on the ground with your eyes closed, taking nice deep breaths and exhaling down to the Earth will help you to feel very present, strong, stable and connected to your Earth Star Chakra. You even might feel tingling in the bottoms of your feet as the Earth sends you love, healing and grounding to her.

Our bodies are a part of all the Earth's treasures, and feeling grass beneath your feet or dirt between your toes can be a fun way to play with the magic of Mother nature.

Connecting to her will make you strong.

Words for the Earth Star Chakra:
Stability, Nature, Grounding, Calm

Root Chakra

Our true power comes from within us, and from

The first Chakra inside your body is called the Root, and it rests at the base of your spine. Bright red, like an apple, the Root Chakra is the energy center that allows us to feel connected to our family, and to our physical world. This Chakra is like the Earth Star, in that it helps us to feel stable and strong, like a tree.

How would it feel to be a strong as a tree? Trees have very long roots that connect to the Earth to allow it to grow tall. If you want to feel like a tree, simply imagine the color red shining brightly in your Root Chakra, and imagine roots from the base of your spine going down into the ground and connecting with your Earth Star Chakra. Your legs can be like a tree trunk, and create a wonderful sensation of balance and strength during challenging moments in your life. Imagine the color red sending healing light all through your lower body, and down into the planet.

What kind of tree do you imagine yourself to be?

the magic of our imagination to create our reality.

Words for the Root Chakra:
Strength, family, responsibility, Earth,
power, Honor, Nature, All is One

Sacral Chakra

Honoring the gifts of emotions will help you to

Have you ever heard of a Navel orange? That is exactly the color and location of your Sacral Chakra. Just below your belly button lies the star that is the source of all your emotions, senses and creativity. It spins bright orange, like a sunset. The Navel Chakra helps us to connect to all of our feelings whether they are happy, sad, angry, embarrassed, frustrated or peaceful. When you are having a very strong feeling about a person or situation, you are connected to the energy of your Sacral Chakra. This energy center also teaches us to live fully in the present moment.

You know how sometimes you feel sad or lonely, and it feels like it may never go away? Focusing on your Sacral Chakra can help you to remember that we are made of many emotions and life experiences, and that the changing cycles of life have a way of healing every situation.

Remember that no feeling last forever and noticing everything beautiful around and inside of you can help you live in the present moment.

experience the full passions of life.

Words for the Sacral Chakra:
Feelings, Relationships, Emotion, Present
Moment, Senses, Express Yourself, Creativity

Solar Plexus Chakra

You were born to shine. Be true to yourself and celebrate

Your next Chakra is named for the brightest star in the sky. Like the Sun that showers you with warmth and light, your Solar Plexus Chakra dances with its yellow glow in the middle of your body.

In your belly, just between your ribs the Solar Plexus Chakra is pulsing to the rhythms of all that makes you unique. Your special gifts of courage are stored here, and like the Suns rays the creative parts of your personality burst forth in dazzling waves. Your Solar Plexus is filled with the energy of will power, patience and determination to help you find your special place in the world. It is the Chakra that inspires your dreams to come alive.

Would you like to know how to connect to this extraordinary energy? Close your eyes and feel the radiant yellow glow of the Sun warming your body from your belly to your toes. Then send brilliant waves of light through your heart and out the top of your head. Know that you shine like the brightest star in the sky. Let the light fill you with the power to be courageous, confident and uniquely you.

everything that makes you unique.

Words for the Solar Plexus Chakra:
Will power, Determination, Self Esteem,
Patience, Creativity, Integrity, Honor Oneself

Heart Chakra

Loving yourself is the

The next Chakra is a very special star, and contains our feelings of love. The emotions that connect us to every other being, including compassion, joy and forgiveness are held in this very important space. The color of your Heart Chakra is green, like a lush garden or a forest. This is also the energy center that connects the four lower Chakras, to the three higher ones.

Place your hand over your heart and feel the beating of love and life in your chest. The Heart is what allows us to have empathy and compassion for other people's emotions. Sometimes it can feel like an ache, and even make you want to cry. Feeling other people's troubles and wanting to help them to feel better means you have connected to the energy of your Heart Chakra. Naturally, happy feelings arise from this place as well, like the feeling of being hugged by Mom or Dad or being with your best friend.

Of course, the most important person to love is your very own sweet self. Remember that you are a star, unique and beautiful. You are love.

gateway to loving all of life.

Words for the Heart Chakra:
Love, Compassion. Healing, Empathy, Self-care, Kindness, Understanding

Throat Chakra

Think of the blue sky on a summer day and

When you think of the Chakra in the Throat, remember the words speak and silence. Although they seem like two very different things, in this star they share the same space. In your throat, sparkling like a sapphire, or the reflection off a deep blue lake lives your ability to both speak your truth and listen with your own inner voice. Have you ever said "yes" when you really meant "no?" Have you ever wanted to speak up but felt afraid or unsure to use your voice? This Chakra gives you the strength to be heard. There may be times you feel anxious about sharing your thoughts and ideas. You may be afraid of being criticized, or you may feel like using your voice to criticize or hurt others. You may not feel brave enough to tell the truth. This is where the gift of silence can help.

Learning to recognize your own inner voice can help you to choose your words with love and kindness. This blue jewel can give you the confidence to speak up without the fear of what others might think. It can help you to think twice about saying something hurtful to a friend, or forgive a friend who has said unkind words to you. The inner voice can only be heard when you take the time to be silent and listen with your Heart. Your inner voice is filled with integrity, lighting the way to choose your words with wisdom.

write a loving message to you

Words for the Throat Chakra:
Speak Your Truth, Be Heard, Silent
Inner Voice, Speak With Integrity

Brow Chakra

With my eyes closed I see everything I need

Have you ever heard the phone ring, and knew who was calling before you said hello? Have you ever had a hunch and found out later you were exactly right? This is the gift of the Brow Chakra. The gift of intuition. It is sometimes called a third eye, and it rests in the center of your forehead, between your eyebrows.

The thought of having a third eye might sound a little strange, but here lies the source of your intuition and natural wisdom. Purple is the color of this extraordinary energy center, and connecting with it is as simple as meditating for a few minutes each day. Just close your eyes, relax, and slowly breath in and out.

The color purple may appear in your third eye... do not give up if it does not happen right away. We are all born with a sense of intuition. Practice, patience and time are keys to unlocking the gifts of the third eye. Using your intuition makes you aware and makes you wise. Quieting your mind for a little while each day allows your inner knowing to activate, and lets you hear what your body has to say. Close your eyes and imagine a brilliant violet light. Breathe deep into your body and relax into yourself.

to see, I let my inner vision guide me.

Words for the Brow Chakra:
Quiet Mind, Inspirations, Inner Knowing,
Intuition, Stillness, Trust Yourself

Crown Chakra

What colors do you see when you think of

Our journey through your Body of Stars is almost complete. The last star is the crowning glory of your energy system and is located at the very top of your head. This mystical opening acts as a funnel mixing all the beautiful colors together to create White Light.

It is called the Crown Chakra, and it is the gateway that connects you to the grace and glory of Spirit; to God. This energy center encourages you to seek and strengthen your Spirituality by linking your intentions to the infinite light from the Divine. Through meditation and stillness your heart opens a pathway up through the top of your head, connecting with the Divine. This beam of illumination descends from the heavens and floods your crown with healing light. The glow that surrounds you is filled with peace and boundless love.

When the problems of life build up inside of us we can send them out the tops of our heads and into the light where they can be handled by God and our Angels. We can also send joy and gratitude, for the Universe loves and needs all that is positive and filled with joy. Allow the light to penetrate your Crown Chakra and let it help you to know you are loved and complete simply because you exist.

the Crown Chakra?

Words for the Crown Chakra:
Divine Guidance, Faith, Meditation,
Grace, Prayer, Gratitude, Illumination

Create your own Chakra Mobile

Craft items:
- color crayons
- vegetable oil
- small bowl
- small brush
- scissors
- thread or fine string
- needle or hole punch, to create a small hole

With your adult helper, gently cut the 8 black and white Chakra images out of along the edges. Color each Chakra, front and back, with the crayons in the colors that feel best to you. Dab the paint brush in a small bowl filled with vegetable oil, and brush both sides of the Chakras. The oil will give your mobile a stained glass effect. You may want to place them on a covered surface, undisturbed, to dry.

When the oil is completely dry (will take several hours), start with the Earth Star Chakra. Have your adult helper use a needle or hole punch to poke a small hole in the top, to string thread through. Create a small hole in the bottom of the Root Chakra and string the thread up to it. Leave a few inches of thread between the Chakras. Tie a small knot between the Chakras to seal off the loop.

Repeat by creating a small hole in the top of the Root Chakra, and connecting the thread to the bottom of the Sacral Chakra. Tie off the loop. From the top of the Sacral, continue on up to the bottom of the Solar Plexus, etc., until you have strung them all together to form a mobile.

When you get to the Crown Chakra, you may want to make a small hole in the top, place enough thread to create a way to hang your mobile in a special place!

Earth Star

Root

Turn the page, there's more!

Sacral

Solar

About the Author & Illustrator

Author

Ameera Beth is an Atlantean High Priestess, living in the Pacific Northwest. She serves as a healer and channel for the dolphins, whales and the Mer beings. She considers the Merfolk to be her family, and is a conduit for others to connect with their body as energy, and the energy of Atlantis. Ameera feels it is especially important for parents to have resources to teach their children about the Chakras and the energy that flows within and around them.

For more information on classes or to receive a private Trans-Personal Healing session, find her at www.dolphinmoonhealing.com or ameerabeth@dolphinmoonhealing.com.

Illustrator

Chloe Metcalf is an Australian empathic intuitive artist who has been channeling art and messages from universal guides for almost half a decade. She currently teaches spiritual basics to many people around the world guiding many on their journey, working primarily with the crystal and rainbow children. Chloe is writing/crafting her own books for all ages. Chloe draws for inspiration from her past lives and higher self for inspiration and has been an artist since about the age of 8.

Reach her at her Facebook page https://www.facebook.com/ChloeMetcalfIntuitiveArtist

Made in the USA
San Bernardino, CA
30 October 2015